Elizabeth I

Andrew Langley

Illustrated by Mark Bergin

 Heinemann

HISTORY OF BRITAIN – ELIZABETH I
was produced for Heinemann Children's Reference
by Lionheart Books, London

First published in Great Britain by Heinemann
Children's Reference, an imprint of Heinemann
Educational Publishers, a division of Reed
Educational and Professional Publishing Limited,
Halley Court, Jordan Hill, Oxford OX2 8EJ

MADRID ATHENS
FLORENCE PRAGUE WARSAW
PORTSMOUTH NH CHICAGO SAO PAULO MEXICO
SINGAPORE TOKYO MELBOURNE AUCKLAND
IBADAN GABORONE JOHANNESBURG KAMPALA NAIROBI

Editors: Lionel Bender, Sue Reid
Designer: Ben White
Editorial Assistant: Madeleine Samuel
Picture Researcher: Jennie Karrach
Media Conversion: Peter MacDonald
Typesetting: R & B Partnership

Educational Consultant: Jane Shuter
Editorial Advisors: Andrew Farrow, Paul Shuter

Production Controller: David Lawrence
Editorial Director: David Riley

ISBN 0 600 58836 X Hb
ISBN 0 600 58837 8 Pb

British Library Cataloguing-in-Publication Data.
A catalogue record for this book is available from
the British Library.

Printed in Italy

Acknowledgements
Picture Credits
FI = Fotomas Index, NPG = National Portrait Gallery, London, BAL =
Bridgeman Art Library. RHPL = Robert Harding Picture Library.
t = top, b = bottom, l = left, r = right, c = centre.
Page 4bl: The Royal Collection © 1996 Her Majesty the Queen Elizabeth II.
5tl: The Mansell Collection. 5tr: Public Record Office SP/11/4 no.2. 5b:
NPG4451. 6c: British Library. 6b: NPG362. 7t: FI. 7b: NPG5175. 8tr:
National Library of Scotland ACC9309.f22. 8b: Scottish National Portrait
Gallery. 9cr: FI. 9b: Penshurst Place, Kent. 10t: Mary Evans Picture
Library. 10c: Ashmolean Museum, Oxford. 10-11b: Public Record Office
MPF 366/1. 11t: FI. 12tr: Historic Scotland. 12bl: NPG2162. 13t:
NPG447. 13b: Bodleian Library, Oxford MS Ashmole.1729, fol 13r. 14t:
Mary Evans Picture Library. 14c: FI. 15t: NPG4032. 16t: By kind permis-
sion of His Grace the Duke of Norfolk and the Baroness Herries. 16bl:
NPG4106. 16br: British Library. 18-19 Michael Holford. 19cr: National
Maritime Museum D3301. 19bl, br: FI. 20cl, 20tr: FI. 20: BAL/Private
Collection. 21: Corsham Court, no.22/Unichrome (Bath) Ltd. 22c: From
His Grace, Duke of Atholl's Collection, Blair Castle, Perthshire. 22b:
BAL/British Library, London.
All artwork by Mark Bergin except map page 23, by Hayward Art
Group.
Cover: Artwork by Mark Bergin. Photographs: William Cecil portrait
(National Portrait Gallery), Spanish Armada (Michael Holford), Rosary (By
permission of His Grace the Duke of Norfolk and the Baroness Herries).

Every effort has been made to contact copyright holders of any material
reproduced in this book. Any omissions or errors will be rectified in subse-
quent printings if notice is given to the Publisher.

PLACES TO VISIT

Here are some sites and museums which have connections with Elizabeth I and her times. Your local tourist office may be able to tell you about other places to visit in your area.

Burghley House, Cambridgeshire. Home of the Cecil family, built by Lord Burghley.

Elizabethan House, Plymouth, Devon. Exhibits showing the daily life of the typical Elizabethan.

Hardwick Hall, Derbyshire. This beautiful Elizabethan house was completed in 1597.

Hatfield House, Hertfordshire. The queen spent much time here as a child. Today it contains many of her belongings, including hat, gloves and stockings.

Hever Castle, Kent. This was Anne Boleyn's family home. It has many objects associated with her and Elizabeth.

Holyroodhouse, Edinburgh. Palace where Mary Stuart lived as queen and prisoner.

Kenilworth Castle, Warwickshire. The ruins of the home of Robert Dudley, visited three times by Elizabeth.

Knole, Kent. Good for the study of the daily life of important gentry.

National Maritime Museum, Greenwich. Paintings and relics of many ships, including those of the Armada.

National Portrait Gallery, London. Houses pictures of many notable Elizabethans.

Ormondes Castle, Tipperary, Eire. The supposed birthplace of Anne Boleyn.

Sherborne Castle, Dorset. The ruins of the home of Sir Walter Raleigh, with a collection of paintings.

Stratford-on-Avon, Warwickshire. Shakespeare's birthplace.

Tower of London. Scene of many episodes in Elizabeth's life, with plenty of treasures on show.

Westminster Abbey, London. Crownings and burials of monarchs.

INTRODUCTION

King Henry VIII wanted a son to inherit his throne. But his wife, Catherine of Aragon, only had one child that lived, a daughter, Mary. The king divorced her, and married the bewitching Anne Boleyn. On 7 September 1533, the new queen had a baby. It was another daughter. Henry was bitterly disappointed. He believed that girls were not suitable to be rulers.

But he was utterly wrong. His second child grew up to become Elizabeth I, the strongest and cleverest of all the queens of Britain. During her reign, the country became peaceful and united after years of unrest, and beat back the threat of a Spanish invasion.

CONTENTS

Princess in Peril

In spite of his disappointment, the king was very proud of his youngest daughter. He often carried her about, and showed her off to his courtiers. But the young Elizabeth spent most of her early life far away from the court, at Hatfield Palace in Hertfordshire.

By 1536, it was clear that Anne Boleyn would not have a son. Henry wanted to be rid of her. She was accused of having love affairs with other men, and beheaded. The king swiftly married Jane Seymour. Within a few months, a royal prince, Edward, was born. He was to be the next ruler.

Meanwhile, Elizabeth was growing up into a pretty and intelligent girl. She was quick to learn many subjects, from geography and astronomy to dancing and horse-riding.

▽ **The Princess Elizabeth arrives at the river gate of the Tower of London** in 1554. At first, she sat on the steps in the pouring rain and refused to go in, fearing she might be executed. Then one of her male servants began to cry, and Elizabeth took pity on him by entering the Tower. After two months, Mary sent her to Woodstock in Oxfordshire.

◁**Lady Jane Grey was a great-granddaughter of Henry VII.** She was also a Protestant. Edward wanted a Protestant to rule after him. He wrote a will naming Lady Jane Grey as his heir.

On Edward's death, Jane was made queen. But Mary refused to accept this. She rode to London and, despite her religion, had the support of the people because she was Henry's eldest daughter. Lady Jane Grey was put in the Tower. Later, she was beheaded. She was Queen of England for only nine days.

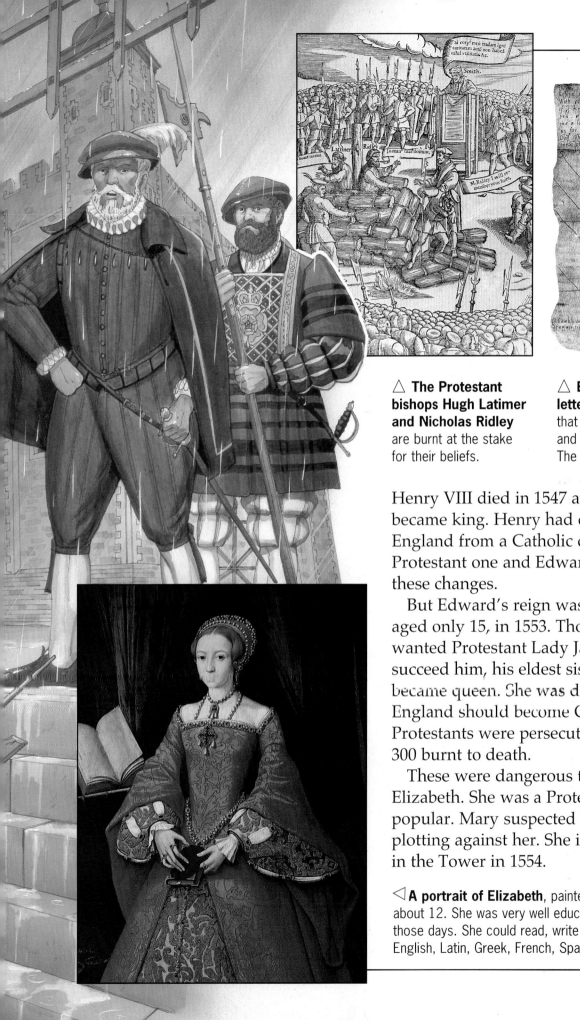

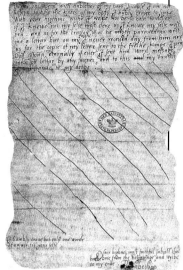

△ **The Protestant bishops Hugh Latimer and Nicholas Ridley** are burnt at the stake for their beliefs.

△ **Elizabeth wrote this letter to Mary**, insisting that she was innocent, and begging for a reply. The queen refused.

Henry VIII died in 1547 and Edward became king. Henry had changed England from a Catholic country to a Protestant one and Edward continued these changes.

But Edward's reign was brief. He died, aged only 15, in 1553. Though he had wanted Protestant Lady Jane Grey to succeed him, his eldest sister Mary became queen. She was determined that England should become Catholic again. Protestants were persecuted and nearly 300 burnt to death.

These were dangerous times for Elizabeth. She was a Protestant and very popular. Mary suspected Elizabeth of plotting against her. She imprisoned her in the Tower in 1554.

◁ **A portrait of Elizabeth**, painted when she was about 12. She was very well educated for a girl in those days. She could read, write and speak in English, Latin, Greek, French, Spanish and Welsh.

THE NEW QUEEN

On the night of 17 November 1558, the bells of London rang out. The people "did eat and drink and make merry". There were two reasons to celebrate: hated Queen Mary was dead, and the new queen was to be the young and much-loved Elizabeth.

▷ **A map of the centre of Tudor London.** It shows part of the route followed by Elizabeth's procession in 1559. She travelled from the Tower, through the City to Westminster, where Parliament sat. Next day, she was crowned in Westminster Abbey.

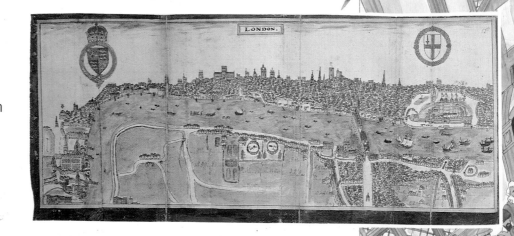

Elizabeth was told the news as she sat under an oak tree at Hatfield. At once, she hurried to London to be crowned.

But, although she was so popular, she still had to be careful. The kings of France and Spain, both Catholic countries, wanted to stamp out the Protestant faith in England. They might invade if she seemed weak.

Also, most people believed that women were too weak to govern a country. They urged Elizabeth to marry, so that England could be ruled by a man.

The queen moved cautiously. She chose wise and experienced men for her team of closest advisors, the Privy Council. She pushed new laws through Parliament which made England firmly Protestant. The monarch now became Supreme Governor of the Church. Priests had to use the new English Prayer Book.

▽ **William Cecil, Lord Burghley** (1520-1598), was Elizabeth's Secretary of State, and her most trusted and important minister.

▷ **Elizabeth on her way to be crowned.** Parts of the coronation service were spoken in English. Catholics used only Latin. The changes were to show that England was now a Protestant land.

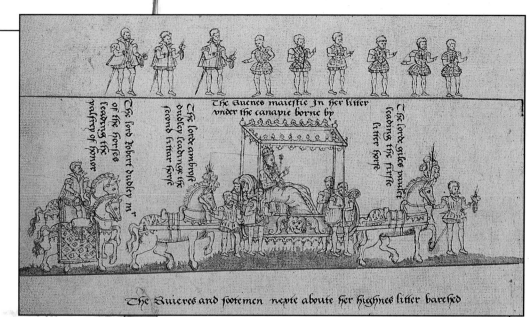

Elizabeth showed quickly that she was a strong ruler. The Spanish ambassador wrote that she was "more feared than her sister, and has her way as absolutely as her father did". He hoped that she would marry his master, King Philip II.

Several other European kings wanted to wed Elizabeth and gain control of England. But the queen was in no hurry to marry. She preferred to spend most of her time with her favourite courtier, the dashing Lord Robert Dudley.

◁ **Children watch Elizabeth's coronation procession (far left).** She is being carried in a litter supported by horses. Footmen with pikes escort the litter as the procession moves through the streets. Elizabeth often stopped to talk to spectators.

◁ **The queen in her coronation robes.** She is wearing a crown and holding the orb (globe) and sceptre (staff), symbols of her power.

TROUBLE WITH SCOTLAND

Elizabeth's most dangerous rival was her cousin, Mary Stuart. Mary was Catholic. She was also the Queen of Scotland and married to the King of France. Many Catholics believed that Mary had a stronger claim to England's throne than Elizabeth.

When Mary's husband died in 1560, she left France and went back to Scotland. This was a Protestant land. Few Scots wanted a Catholic queen. But Mary quickly charmed her new subjects. She even rode with her army to put down a Catholic rebellion in 1562.

At that moment came the first great crisis of Elizabeth's reign. She caught smallpox, a disease which killed many people in those times. For several days she lay close to death at Hampton Court. Her ministers were terrified that she would die before she could name an heir. This might lead to civil war.

Luckily, Elizabeth survived the disease, though her face was marked with smallpox scars ever afterwards. When she had recovered, her anxious Parliament begged her to marry as soon as possible. Then she might have children who would succeed her.

Elizabeth gave only a vague answer. She told Parliament that she was still young enough to marry and bear children, but had no definite plans yet.

▷ **Mary, Queen of Scots, with her cousin Henry Stuart, Lord Darnley.** Mary quickly fell in love with the handsome Darnley, and the pair married in 1565. But it was a miserable marriage. Darnley turned out to be a drunkard and a bully.

▷ **An early portrait of Mary, Queen of Scots.** Her father was King James V of Scotland. He died only a week after she was born, in 1542. Because Scotland and England were then at war, the infant queen was sent to live in the safety of the French court. Her mother ruled Scotland as regent in her place.

Meanwhile, the threat from Mary grew. Several foreign rulers wanted to marry her. Elizabeth feared that this would be dangerous for England. So in 1564 she suggested that her own favourite, Robert Dudley, Earl of Leicester, should marry Mary. This would force her to be loyal to Elizabeth. But by then it was too late. Mary was already in love with another handsome nobleman, Lord Darnley. In July 1565, Darnley was declared King of Scotland. The next day they were married.

◁ **Elizabeth lies dangerously ill with smallpox.** Her German doctor used a medieval cure. This involved medicines and wrapping the queen from head to foot in scarlet cloth.

△ **Scotsman John Knox** (1513-1572) was a stern and fiery Protestant preacher. He angered Elizabeth, by saying that women should not rule. He angered Mary, by condemning her marriage.

◁ **The queen dancing** with her favourite courtier, Robert Dudley.

MARRIAGE PLANS

**"I really believe that the queen will never marry",
said the Earl of Leicester in 1566. It seemed that he
was right. Elizabeth saw clearly that any marriage
might weaken her own power and the affection of her
people. She told her councillors: "I am already bound
unto a husband, which is the Kingdom of England."**

All the same, she flirted with several
foreign princes. The most important of
these was the Archduke Charles of
Austria. He would be a strong ally
against Spain and France. The archduke
was eager to marry and sent an envoy to
visit the English queen. But Elizabeth
kept him waiting with vague promises.
Eventually, Charles married his niece.

Other offers of marriage were easier to
refuse. One was from the King of France,
but he was only fourteen years old.
Another came from Ivan 'the Terrible',
the bloodthirsty Tsar of Russia. He
suggested that Elizabeth should live in
Moscow, to be safe from assassins!

Yet again, Parliament begged the
queen to decide on a husband. She was
furious that the matter was discussed in
public. "Is not my kingdom here?" she
demanded. "Though I be a woman, yet
I have as good a courage as ever my
father had."

Elizabeth had only to look at Scotland
to see how an unwise marriage could
lead to disaster. There, Mary had quickly
grown to hate her husband, and had a
new favourite, her secretary David
Riccio. In March 1566, Riccio was
stabbed to death by the jealous Darnley
and his supporters.

▷ **Archduke Charles
of Austria (above
right)**, son of the Holy
Roman Emperor.

△ **Riding gloves.** The
queen was a bold and
skilful horsewoman.

▷ **A rough sketch of
the scene of Lord
Darnley's murder** at
Kirk o'Field. Mary left
him alone here on the
night of 9 February
1567. Early next
morning, a huge
explosion wrecked the
house. The bodies of
Darnley and his servant
(shown top right) were
found in a nearby
garden. Mary's baby son
James is shown top left.

◁ **Elizabeth sits in Parliament.** She needed the agreement of the members to raise money through taxation.

▷ **Elizabeth addresses the House of Lords.** When she was angry, she reminded the older nobles of her father.

Worse was to come. Early in 1567, Darnley was murdered. Many suspected Mary of plotting his death with her lover, the Earl of Bothwell. When she married him, the Scots were outraged. Rebels defeated Mary's army, and in 1568 she was forced to flee to England for safety, leaving her son behind.

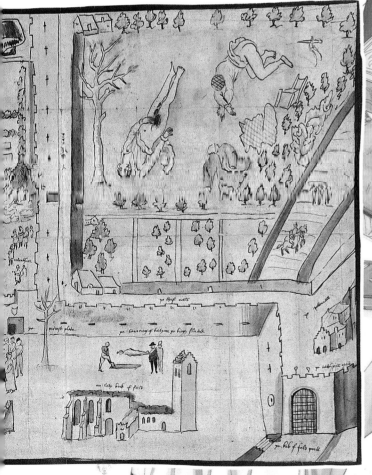

PLOTS AND REBELLION

Mary was now an even bigger threat to Elizabeth. Disgraced in Scotland, she had to stay in England. But it was too dangerous to allow her to remain at liberty. Elizabeth ordered that she should be kept in Tutbury Castle, a remote stronghold in Staffordshire.

▽ **Holyroodhouse in Edinburgh.** Mary, Queen of Scots lived here until her exile. This sketch plan was drawn by an English spy.

One of the queen's most trusted councillors was the Duke of Norfolk. In 1569, Elizabeth was horrified to hear that the duke planned to marry Mary. He denied it, saying that he would never marry "so wicked a woman".

All the same, Norfolk was mixed up in a plot by northern Catholic nobles. That November, they raised an army and marched south, to try and rescue Mary.

▽ **Sir Christopher Hatton** was Elizabeth's most faithful courtier. He loved her so much that he stayed unmarried until his death.

▽ **Burghley's officers arrest servants of the Duke of Norfolk** as the Ridolfi Plot is unmasked in 1571. Roberto Ridolfi was an Italian banker. Suspicion began when he sent news about his plans to English friends. The messenger was arrested and his letters seized. Then spies discovered that Norfolk was sending money to Mary's supporters in Scotland, and searched his house.

◁ **Robert Dudley (1532-1588)** had been a friend of Elizabeth's since childhood. On her accession, he came to court and became the queen's favourite. Many people feared that she would marry him when his wife died in mysterious circumstances. Dudley was made Earl of Leicester in 1564.

The rebels captured Durham, and urged all Catholics to join them. But by now troops loyal to Elizabeth were heading north to oppose them. The rebels lost their nerve, and most of them retreated into Scotland. The rest were defeated.

Elizabeth took a furious revenge, ordering 750 rebels to be put to death. Norfolk was spared. But he joined a fresh plot to rescue Mary, led by Roberto Ridolfi. According to Ridolfi's wild plan, Spanish troops would invade England and assassinate Elizabeth. The plot was uncovered in autumn 1571. Norfolk was arrested and placed in the Tower.

◁ **A hastily scribbled letter from the queen to Lord Burghley**, cancelling the execution of the Duke of Norfolk in April 1572. He had been found guilty of treason for his part in the Ridolfi Plot, but Elizabeth kept delaying his death. Eventually, the House of Commons demanded the duke's head. He was executed on 2 June.

DRIFTING TO WAR

In 1572 Britain and France, despite their religious differences, made an agreement to help each other if attacked by another country. As a sign of the new friendship, Elizabeth was urged yet again to marry – this time to the French Duke of Alençon.

FRANCISCVS HERCVLES HENRICI·III·FRAN·
CORVM REGIS FRATER·DVX ALENCONIVS.
Antverpie apud Petri de Iode.

▷ **An engraving of the queen in an idealized country setting**, surrounded by peasants and court ladies with musical instruments. It comes from *Aprill*, one of the poems in Edmund Spenser's *Shepherd's Calendar* published in 1579. The whole poem is in honour of the queen, who is called 'Fair Eliza'. Spenser later wrote *The Faerie Queene*.

△ **Francis, Duke of Alençon.** His plan to marry Elizabeth was ruined after French Catholics massacred about 8,000 Protestants in 1572. The duke's mother, Catherine, probably encouraged the slaughter.

As usual, Elizabeth moved slowly. It was not until 1579 that Alençon came on a secret visit to England. He was only 23, very short and pockmarked, but the queen was enchanted. She called him 'My Frog', and showered him with gifts.

But the match was unpopular. Many of the English hated the French for their harsh treatment of Protestants. They feared that marriage with Alençon would help the Catholic cause in England. Elizabeth sadly realized that she must remain single.

Meanwhile, war was looming with Spain. Spanish power had grown immense. By 1580 Spain ruled Portugal and most of the Netherlands.

Now the Spaniards looked towards England. King Philip had promised the Pope that he would put Mary on the English throne. Spanish troops under the Duke of Parma were already massed on the Dutch coast. Others took part in a Catholic expedition to try and destroy English rule in Ireland.

Philip was also furious with the daring raids of English sailors, especially Francis Drake. Most of Spain's huge wealth came from South and Central America. Galleons carried gold, silver and jewels across the Atlantic to Spain. But during the 1570s Drake had plundered these ships and brought the treasure back to England.

◁ **Sir Francis Drake**
(1543-1596). Drake
waged an unofficial
war against Spanish
shipping for over
20 years.

◁ **The queen knights
Francis Drake** on the
deck of his ship *Golden
Hind* after he became
the first Englishman to
sail round the world.
Elizabeth's share of the
spoils (£160,000) was
enough to cover her
government's expenses
for a whole year.

THE DEATH OF MARY

"I hope to see her head set on a pole, for she is a serpent and a viper!" With this boast, a Catholic fanatic set out to assassinate Elizabeth in 1582. Luckily, he was soon arrested. But there were other plots against the queen's life.

Traitors seemed to be everywhere. The queen's Principal Secretary, Sir Francis Walsingham, built up a network of spies. They watched anyone who might have dealings with Catholic countries. In 1583, Walsingham's men arrested Francis Throckmorton. Under torture, he revealed a plot in which French troops would invade England and free Mary. Elizabeth's life was in real danger. The Pope had declared that the person who assassinated her would be rewarded in Heaven. Angry at this, Parliament hunted down many Catholic priests. Several were condemned to death.

◁ **A rosary, cross and prayer book** carried by Mary at her execution.

▷ **A miniature portrait of Sir Walter Raleigh**, painted by Nicholas Hilliard. Raleigh (1552-1618) came to court in 1581 and quickly became one of the queen's favourites. He was witty, handsome and charming, as well as being a fine soldier and poet. In 1587 he was made Captain of the Guard. This made him responsible for Elizabeth's safety. In 1601, he advised the queen to execute the Earl of Essex, who had rebelled against her.

▽ **Mary is put on trial** at Fotheringhay Castle in October 1586.

Mary was at the centre of all these schemes. Even though she was moved from one castle to another, she still managed to get coded messages to the French ambassador.

Aware of this, Walsingham set a trap for Mary. His spies got hold of her messages, worked out the secret code and read them. Then they passed them on. Mary suspected nothing.

At first, the letters were innocent enough. Then, in June 1586, came a note from Sir Anthony Babington, a wealthy young Catholic. He outlined a plot to kill Elizabeth and for a foreign force to invade England. Mary replied that she welcomed the plan, as long as she could be rescued after Elizabeth's death.

This was the end. The plotters were arrested and executed. Mary herself was tried and found guilty of treason.

◁ **Mary, Queen of Scots is beheaded at Fotheringhay in 1587.** For months, Elizabeth had refused to sign the death warrant. She did not want to execute a fellow monarch. At last, on 1 February, she signed it. Burghley and the other councillors, afraid that she might change her mind, had the sentence carried out as quickly as possible.

On the morning of 18 February, Mary was led to the block on a wooden stage. After the axe had fallen, the executioner picked up her head and shouted: "God save the Queen!"

17

The Armada

"What a valiant woman! She braves the two greatest kings by land and sea!" said the Pope in 1587. He was one of Elizabeth's biggest enemies. But he was right. English troops were fighting the Spanish in the Netherlands. France had allied itself with Spain.

△ **The Battle of Gravelines.** Spanish and English ships blaze away at each other during the eight-hour fight off the Flemish coast.

◁ **The queen rides among her soldiers at Tilbury**, as they wait for the expected Spanish invasion. She declared: "I know I have the body of a weak and feeble woman; but I have the heart and stomach of a king ... and think it foul scorn that Parma or Spain should dare to invade the borders of my realm."

Philip of Spain was so enraged by Mary's execution that he decided to invade England. He assembled a huge fleet, or Armada, in Cadiz harbour. Its job was to sail to the Netherlands and carry the Duke of Parma's soldiers over to England.

But in 1587, Drake made a surprise attack. His ships burst into Cadiz and sank 30 Spanish galleons. "I have singed the king of Spain's beard", he boasted.

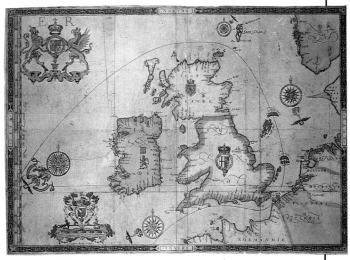

▽ **Playing cards (below) showing scenes from the Armada defeat.** (Left) The queen consults the commanders of her defending fleet. (Right) The queen at a service of thanksgiving in St Paul's for victory over the Spanish. The flags of her navy are proudly displayed.

▷ **A map showing the Armada's route (right).** After the Battle of Gravelines, the Spaniards tried to return to Spain by sailing round Scotland and the west coast of Ireland. But the ships were battered by storms and many sank. Hundreds of men died from disease. Of the 130 ships which set out, only 40 reached home.

Drake's brilliant action delayed the Spanish fleet. When it set out in July 1588, the English were well prepared. As the Armada sailed up the English Channel, it was attacked by ships led by the English commander, Lord Howard.

The Spanish reached Calais, where they dropped anchor. Howard sent in blazing fireships, which so terrified the Spaniards that they cut their anchors. Attacked by the English, the Armada drifted along to Gravelines. Here the ships were hit by a bad storm. Without their anchors they could not keep together. The battered Armada fled for home. England was safe from invasion.

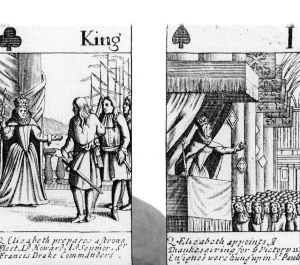

King

Q. Elizabeth prepares a strong Fleet, L? Howard, L? Seymor, S? Francis Drake Commanders.

Q. Elizabeth appoints A Thanksgiving for y Victory u Ensignes were hung up in S? Paul.

GLORIANA

By the early 1590s, Elizabeth was growing old. She was still energetic, dancing six 'galliards' each morning. But she was losing her looks. Her hair was covered with a red wig and her face was coated with make-up. Many of her teeth were black with decay.

Even so, her people and courtiers loved her more than ever. The queen was worshipped almost as a goddess. She was a symbol of Protestant England, defying the might of Spain and France. Poets celebrated her long reign in verse. Among them was Edmund Spenser, whose great work *The Faerie Queene* was finished in 1596. The 'Queene' of the title was called Gloriana (Glory), an image of Elizabeth herself.

Her court became a centre for musicians, playwrights and artists. Two of England's finest composers, Thomas Tallis and William Byrd, worked at the Chapel Royal. Elizabeth had her own company of actors, the Queen's Men. Nicholas Hilliard painted miniature portraits of Elizabeth and several of her courtiers.

△ **William Shakespeare (1564-1616).** The 1590s saw the start of a great age of English drama, led by Shakespeare, Ben Jonson and Christopher Marlowe.

▽ **The queen is carried by her courtiers** through the streets of London in 1600. She is brilliantly dressed in her favourite colours of white and silver. Elizabeth loved fine clothes and jewels.

△ **An illustration from about 1600 honouring Elizabeth.** The circle represents the Solar System as known then, with Elizabeth's qualities, such as wisdom, listed as names of the planets. The outer ring names her as queen of England, France and Scotland.

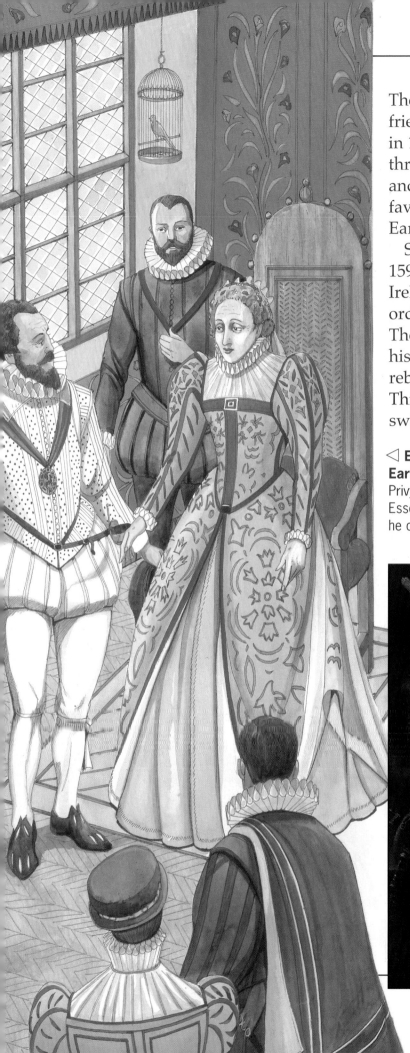

The queen was also losing her closest friends and advisors. Leicester had died in 1588, and Hatton and Walsingham three years later. Burghley was ageing and ill. But Elizabeth had a new favourite – the handsome and arrogant Earl of Essex, 34 years younger than her.

She made him a military leader and in 1599 sent him to put down a revolt in Ireland. But Essex failed to carry out his orders and returned home in disgrace. The angry queen sent him to prison. On his release in 1601, Essex tried to start a rebellion in London against Elizabeth. This, too, was a failure, and he was swiftly tried and executed.

◁ **Elizabeth with the Earl of Essex** in her Privy (private) Chamber. Essex wrongly thought he could bully the queen.

▽ **A portrait of the queen painted after her death.** Only now could portrait painters show her as old.

END OF AN AGE

In November 1601, Elizabeth made one of her last speeches to Parliament. She said, "Though you have had, and may have, many princes more mighty and wise sitting in this seat, yet you never had, nor shall have, any that will be more careful and loving".

▽ **Mary, Queen of Scots with her son James.** He became King of Scotland in 1567, and King James I of England after Elizabeth's death.

That year, the queen also made her last official tour. She still seemed full of energy, often riding as far as 15 kilometres a day. And she was still able to terrify ministers. But by early 1603, now aged nearly 70, she began to grow feeble. She ate little, and sat huddled on cushions. She died on 24 March.

A month later, her coffin was carried through London. Most people wept to see the end of their beloved queen, whose reign had lasted for nearly 45 years. When it began, England was poor, weak and divided. Under Elizabeth, trade and industry grew, Spain was defeated, and the Protestant church was firmly established. The country became one of the strongest and most peaceful in the world.

▽ **The queen's coffin is drawn by horses to her funeral, followed by 1,600 mourners.** A painted, life-size image of the queen can be seen on top of her coffin. The coffin had come by boat on the Thames from Richmond to Whitehall. There it was placed on a carriage and taken to Westminster Abbey. Knights and courtiers held a canopy and banners over it.

GLOSSARY

ambassador an official who represents a country overseas.

assassinate to murder an important public figure.

astronomy the study of the stars and planets.

Catholic a Christian who believes that the Pope is head of the Church and does what he says.

court the servants and advisors of a monarch ('courtiers').

El Dorado legendary place in South America, believed to be rich in gold and treasure.

envoy someone who carries a message from one government to another.

exile being sent away from one's native country, and having to live in another.

galleon a large vessel with three masts used as a merchant ship or warship.

galliard a popular and energetic dance, full of leaps and turns.

litter a couch mounted on poles, carried by people or horses.

navigation the science of finding one's way using a compass and a study of the positions of the stars.

Privy Council the body of ministers and other officials who advise the monarch.

Protestant a member of one of the Christian churches which split from the Catholic Church during the Reformation of the 16th century.

regent a person who is given authority to govern a country in place of a monarch who is too young or sick to rule.

rosary a string of beads used by Catholics to count a set of prayers to the Virgin Mary.

smallpox an infectious and sometimes deadly disease which leaves pimples and blisters.

treason the attempt to overthrow or betray a country's government or its ruler.

▷ **Elizabethan England.** This map shows the major cities and towns mentioned in this book, including those listed on page 2.

INDEX